Abbreviations and Symbols

beg . . . . begin(ning)

BL(s) . . . . back loop(s)

BPsc . . . back post single crochet(s)

ch(s) . . . . chain(s)

CL(s) . . . . cluster(s)

dc . . . . double crochet(s)

dec . . . . decrease(-ing)

Fig. . . . . figure

FL(s) . . . . front loop(s)

hdc . . . . half double crochet(s)

lp(s) . . . . loop(s)

patt . . . . pattern

prev . . . . previous

rem . . . . remain(ing)

rep . . . . repeat(ing)

rnd(s) . . . . round(s)

sc . . . . single crochet(s)

sk . . . . skip

sl . . . . slip

sl st(s) . . . . slip stitch(es)

sp(s) . . . . space(s)

st(s) . . . . stitch(es)

tog . . . . together

YO . . . . yarn over

* An asterisk is used to mark the beginning of a portion of instructions to be worked more than once; thus, "rep from ***** twice more" means after working the instructions once, repeat the instructions following the asterisk twice more (3 times in all).

† The dagger identifies a portion of instructions that will be repeated again later in the same row or round.

— The number after a long dash at the end of a row or round indicates the number of stitches you should have when the row or round has been completed. The long dash can also be used to indicate a completed stitch such as a decrease, a shell, or a cluster.

() Parentheses are used to enclose instructions which should be worked the exact number of times specified immediately following the parentheses, such as "(2 sc in next dc, sc in next dc) twice." They are also used to set off and clarify a group of stitches that are to be worked all into the same space or stitch, such as "in next corner sp work (2 dc, ch 1, 2 dc)."

[] Brackets and **()** parentheses are also used to provide additional information to clarify instructions.

Join - join with a sl st unless otherwise specified.

The patterns in this book are written using United States terminology. Terms which have different English equivalents are noted below.

United States	English
single crochet (sc)	double crochet (dc)
half double crochet (hdc)	half treble (htr)
double crochet (dc)	treble (tr)
skip (sk)	miss
slip stitch (sl st) . . . . slip stitch (ss) or ("single crochet")	
gauge	tension
yarn over (YO) . . . . yarn over hook (YOH)	

A Word About Yarns

4-ply worsted weight 100% cotton yarn is used for the projects in this book. The models in this book were made using Bernat® Handicrafter® cotton and Lily Sugar 'n Cream®. Any worsted weight cotton yarn can also be used.
If you cannot find cotton yarn in your area, please write to the publisher for mail order sources.

Gauge

A correct stitch gauge is very important. Please take the time to work a stitch gauge swatch about 4" x 4". Measure the swatch. If the number of stitches and rows are fewer than indicated under "Gauge" in the pattern, your hook is too large. Try another swatch with a smaller hook. If the number of stitches and rows are more than indicated under "Gauge" in the pattern, your hook is too small. Try another swatch with a larger size hook.

Stitch Guide

Chain - ch:
YO, draw through lp on hook.

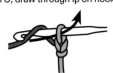

Single Crochet - sc:
Insert hook in st, YO and draw through, YO and draw through both lps on hook.

Half Double Crochet - hdc:
YO, insert hook in st, YO, draw through, YO and draw through all 3 lps on hook.

Double Crochet - dc:
YO, insert hook in st, YO, draw through, (YO and draw through 2 lps on hook) twice.

Triple Crochet - trc:
YO twice, insert hook in st, YO, draw through, (YO and draw through 2 lps on hook) 3 times.

Slip Stitch - sl st:
(a) Used for Joinings
Insert hook in indicated st, YO and draw through st and lp on hook.

(b) Used for Moving Yarn Over
Insert hook in st, YO draw through st and lp on hook.

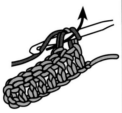

Front Loop - FL:
The front loop is the loop toward you at the top of the stitch.

Back Loop - BL:
The back loop is the loop away from you at the top of the stitch.

Post:
The post is the vertical part of the stitch.

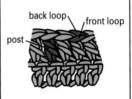

Overcast Stitch is worked loosely to join crochet pieces.

Metric Conversion Charts

INCHES INTO MILLIMETERS & CENTIMETERS (Rounded off slightly)

inches	mm	cm	inches	cm	inches	cm	inches	cm
1/8	3		5	12.5	21	53.5	38	96.5
1/4	6		5 1/2	14	22	56	39	99
3/8	10	1	6	15	23	58.5	40	101.5
1/2	13	1.3	7	18	24	61	41	104
5/8	15	1.5	8	20.5	25	63.5	42	106.5
3/4	20	2	9	23	26	66	43	109
7/8	22	2.2	10	25.5	27	68.5	44	112
1	25	2.5	11	28	28	71	45	114.5
1 1/4	32	3.2	12	30.5	29	73.5	46	117
1 1/2	38	3.8	13	33	30	76	47	119.5
1 3/4	45	4.5	14	35.5	31	79	48	122
2	50	5	15	38	32	81.5	49	124.5
2 1/2	65	6.5	16	40.5	33	84	50	127
3	75	7.5	17	43	34	86.5		
3 1/2	90	9	18	46	35	89		
4	100	10	19	48.5	36	91.5		
4 1/2	115	11.5	20	51	37	94		

mm - millimeter   cm - centimeter

CROCHET HOOKS CONVERSION CHART

U.S.	1/B	2/C	3/D	4/E	5/F	6/G	8/H	9/I	10/J	10 1/2/K
English	12	11	10	9	8	7	6	5	4	2
Continental-mm	2.25	2.75	3.25	3.5	3.75	4.25	5	5.5	6	6.5

Casual Chic (pg.9)

Size:
About 14" tall x 10" wide without strap

Materials:
Worsted weight cotton yarn, 5 oz (250 yds, 150 g) blue;
   2$\frac{1}{2}$ oz (125 yds, 75 g) white and small amounts of red
Note: Solid color version, 5$\frac{1}{2}$ oz (375 yds, 225 g)
Optional for lining, $\frac{1}{3}$ yd fabric; sewing needle and
   matching thread
Size G aluminum crochet hook, or size required
   for gauge

Gauge:
4 dc = 1"

Instructions
Note: Directions are written with color changes for the red, white and blue tote. If a solid color tote is desired, disregard color changes.

Body
With blue, ch 80; join to form a ring, being careful not to twist chain.

Rnd 1 (right side):
Ch 1, sc in same ch as joining and in each rem ch; join in first sc—80 sc.

Rnd 2:
Ch 3 (counts as a dc on this and following rnds), dc in same sc; sk next sc; * 2 dc in next sc; sk next sc; rep from * around; join in 3rd ch of beg ch-3—forty 2-dc groups.

Rnd 3:
Sl st in next dc, ch 3, dc in same dc; * sk next dc, 2 dc in next dc; rep from * around; join in 3rd ch of beg ch-3.

Rnds 4 through 6:
Rep Rnd 3. At end of Rnd 6, change to red by drawing lp through; cut blue.

Rnd 7:
Ch 1, sc in same ch as joining and in each dc; join in first sc. Change to white by drawing lp through; cut red.

Rnd 8:
Sl st in next sc, ch 3, dc in same sc; * sk next sc, 2 dc in next sc; rep from * around; join in 3rd ch of beg ch-3.

Rnds 9 through 12:
Rep Rnd 3. At end of Rnd 12, change to red by drawing lp through; cut white.

Rnd 13:
Ch 1, sc in same ch as joining and in each dc; join in first sc. Change to blue by drawing lp through; cut red.

Rnds 14 through 18:
Rep Rnds 8 through 12. At end of Rnd 18, change to red by drawing lp through; cut blue.

Rnds 19 through 24:
Rep Rnds 7 through 12.

Rnd 25:
Rep Rnd 7. At end of rnd, do not change color. Finish off.

First Strap
Hold body with right side facing you and Rnd 25 at top; join blue in 20th sc of Rnd 25.

Row 1 (right side):
Ch 3 (counts as a dc on this and following rows), dc in same sc; * sk next sc, 2 dc in next sc; rep from * 18 times more—twenty 2-dc groups. Turn, leaving rem sc unworked.

Row 2:
Sk first dc, sl st in next 2 dc, ch 3, dc in same dc as last sl st made; * sk next dc, 2 dc in next dc; rep from * 16 times more—eighteen 2-dc groups. Turn, leaving rem 3 dc unworked.

Row 3:
Sk first dc, sl st in next 2 dc, ch 3, dc in same dc as last sl st made; * sk next dc, 2 dc in next dc; rep from * 14 times more—sixteen 2-dc groups. Turn, leaving rem 3 dc unworked.

Row 4:
Sk first dc, sl st in next 2 dc, ch 3, dc in same dc as last sl st made; * sk next dc, 2 dc in next dc; rep from * 12 times more—fourteen 2-dc groups. Turn, leaving rem 3 dc unworked.

Row 5:
Sk first dc, sl st in next 2 dc, ch 2, dc in same dc as last sl st made—beg cluster made; * sk next dc, keeping last lp of each dc on hook, 2 dc in next dc; YO and draw through all 3 lps on hook—cluster made; rep from * 10 times more—12 clusters. Ch 1, turn.

Row 6:
Sc in next 11 clusters and in next dc. Ch 1, turn, leaving turning ch-2 unworked.

Row 7:
Dec over first 2 sc (to work dec: draw up lp in each of next 2 sc, YO and draw through all 3 lps on hook—dec made); sc in next 8 sc, dec over next 2 sc—10 sc. Ch 1, turn.

Row 8:
Dec over first 2 sc; sc in next 6 sc, dec over next 2 sc—8 sc. Ch 1, turn.

continued

Row 9:
Dec over first 2 sc; sc in next 4 sc, dec over next 2 sc—6 sc. Ch 1, turn.

Row 10:
Sc in each sc. Ch 1, turn.

Rows 11 through 66:
Rep Row 10. At end of Row 66, do not ch 1. Finish off.

Second Strap
Hold body with right side facing you and Rnd 25 at top; sk next sc on Rnd 25 to left of first strap; join blue in next sc.

Row 1 (right side):
Ch 3, dc in same sc; * sk next sc, 2 dc in next sc; rep from * 18 times more—twenty 2-dc groups. Turn.

Rows 2 through 66:
Rep Rows 2 through 66 of first strap. At end of Row 66, do not finish off.

Hold ends of straps with right sides together; working through both thicknesses, sl st through corresponding sc. Finish off.

Turn body inside out with beg ch-80 at top; join blue through both thicknesses in first unused lps of beg ch; working through both thicknesses, sl st in each unused lp. Finish off.

Strap Edging
Hold body with right side facing you; with blue make lp on hook and join with an sc in edge sc on Row 66 of one side of strap; working in sides of rows, sc in next 60 rows, 2 sc in sp formed by edge st on Rows 5 through 1; sc in next sc on Rnd 25 of body, 2 sc in sp formed by edge st on Rows 1 through 5; sc in next 61 rows; join in joining sc. Finish off.

Work edging in same manner on opposite side of strap.

Weave in all ends.

Optional Lining
Step 1:
Cut a rectangle of lining fabric 12" wide by 23" long.

Step 2:
Place 12" ends right sides together and sew with a 1/2" seam for side seam; press seam open. Stitch across one open side for bottom with a 1/2" seam.

Step 3:
On open edge, press 1/2" to the wrong side. Place lining inside the tote with wrong side of lining toward inside of tote. Handstitch the folded edge to inside top edge of tote.

jaunty Shells

Size:
About 12¹/₂" tall x 10¹/₂" wide without strap

Materials:
Worsted weight cotton yarn, 3 oz (150 yds, 90 g) main color; 1 oz (50 yds, 30 g) each of four rainbow colors

Note: Solid color version, 7 oz (350 yds, 210 g)
One contrast color version, 5 oz (250 yds, 150 g) main color; 2 oz (100 yds, 60 g) contrast color

Optional for lining, ¹/₃ yd fabric; sewing needle and matching thread

Size G aluminum crochet hook, or size required for gauge

Gauge:
4 sc = 1"
4 sc rows = 1"

Instructions

Note: Directions are written for color changes for the six multi-colored stripes shown in photograhs on front cover and page 12. If a solid color tote is desired, disregard color changes. If only one contrasting color is used, like photograph on back color, change to that color for stripes 2, 4, and 6.

Starting at bottom with stripe 1 color, ch 4; join to form a ring.

Rnd 1 (right side):
Ch 1, 14 sc in ring; join in first sc—14 sc.

Rnd 2:
Ch 3 (counts as a dc on this and following rnds), dc in same sc as joining; 2 dc in each rem sc; join in 3rd ch of beg ch-3—28 dc.

Rnd 3:
Ch 3, 2 dc in next dc; (dc in next dc, 2 dc in next dc); 13 times; join in 3rd ch of beg ch-3—42 dc.

Rnd 4:
Ch 3, dc in next dc, 2 dc in next dc; (dc in next 2 dc, 2 dc in next dc) 13 times; join in 3rd ch of beg ch-3—56 dc.

Rnd 5:
Ch 3, dc in next 2 dc, 2 dc in next dc; (dc in next 3 dc, 2 dc in next dc) 13 times; join in 3rd ch of beg ch-3—70 dc.

Rnd 6:
Ch 1, 2 sc in same ch as joining; working in BLs only, sc in next 34 dc, 2 sc in next dc; sc in next 34 dc; join in first sc—72 sc. Change to stripe 2 color by drawing lp through; cut yellow.

Rnd 7:
Ch 1, sc in same sc; sk next 2 sc, 7 dc in next sc—shell made; sk next 2 sc; * sc in next sc, sk next 2 sc, 7 dc in next sc—shell made; sk next 2 sc; rep from * 10 times more; join in first sc—12 shells.

Rnd 8:
Ch 3, 6 dc in same sc—beg shell made; sk next 3 dc, sc in next dc, sk next 3 dc; * shell in next sc; sk next 3 dc, sc in next dc, sk next 3 dc; rep from * 10 times more; join in 3rd ch of beg ch-3. Finish off.

Hold piece with right side facing you and Rnd 8 at top; join stripe 3 color in 4th dc of any shell.

Rnd 9:
Ch 1, sc in same dc; sk next 3 dc, shell in next sc; sk next 3 dc; * sc in next dc, sk next 3 dc, shell in next sc; sk next 3 dc; rep from * 10 times more; join in first sc.

Rnd 10:
Beg shell in same sc; sk next 3 dc, sc in next dc, sk next 3 dc; * shell in next sc; sk next 3 dc, sc in next dc, sk next 3 dc; rep from * 10 times more; join in 3rd ch of beg ch-3. Finish off.

Hold piece with right side facing you and Rnd 10 at top; join stripe 4 color in 4th dc of any shell.

Rnds 11 and 12:
Rep Rnds 9 and 10.

Hold piece with right side facing you and Rnd 12 at top; join stripe 5 color in 4th dc of any shell.

Rnds 13 and 14:
Rep Rnds 9 and 10.

Hold piece with right side facing you and Rnd 14 at top; join stripe 6 color in 4th dc of any shell.

Rnds 15 and 16:
Rep Rnds 9 and 10. At end of Rnd 10, change to pink by drawing lp through; cut stripe 6 color.

Note: Rnds 17 through 36 are worked in continuous rnds. Do not join; mark beg of rnds.

Rnd 17:
Ch 1, sc in same ch as joining and in next 6 dc; sk next sc, (sc in next 7 dc, sk next sc) 11 times; do not join—84 sc.

Rnds 18 through 36:
Sc in each sc.

Straps

First Strap:
Row 1 (right side):
Sc in next 18 sc. Ch 1, turn, leaving rem sts unworked.

Row 2:
Sc in first sc, dec over next 2 sc (to work dec: draw up lp in each of next 2 sc, YO and draw through all 3 lps on hook—dec made); sc in each sc to last 3 sc; dec over next 2 sc, sc in last sc—16 sc. Ch 1, turn.

5

continued

Rows 3 through 7:
Rep Row 2. At end of Row 7—6 sc. Ch 1, turn.

Row 8:
Sc in each sc. Ch 1, turn.

Rows 9 through 60:
Rep Row 8. At end of Row 60, finish off.

Second Strap:
Hold piece with right side facing you; with pink make lp on hook and join with an sc in 25th sc from last sc worked on first strap.

Row 1 (right side):
Sc in next 17 sc—18 sc. Ch 1, turn, leaving rem sts unworked.

Rows 2 through 60:
Rep Rows 2 through 60 of first strap. At end of Row 60, do not finish off. Ch 1, turn.

Hold ends of strap with right sides together; working through both thicknesses, sl st through corresponding sc. Finish off.

Edging
Hold tote with right side facing you and one side of strap at top; with pink, make lp on hook and join with an sc in sl st joining of one side of strap; working along side of strap in edge sc, sc in Rows 60 through 1; working across Row 36, sc in next 24 sc; working along side of strap in edge sc, sc in Rows 1 through 60; join in joining sc. Finish off.

Work edging in same manner on opposite side of strap.

Weave in all ends.

Optional Lining
Step 1:
Cut a rectangle of lining fabric 10" wide by 24" long. Cut a circle 6 1/2" in diameter.

Step 2:
Place 10" ends right sides together and sew a 1/2" seam for side seam; press seam open.

Step 3:
Fold the circle in half and then fold again into quarters; mark each quarter along the edge. Also mark one open end of rectangle into quarters. Place lining pieces right sides together, matching the quarter marks; stitch with a 1/2" seam easing rectangle to fit.

Step 4:
On open edge, press 1/2" to the wrong side. Place lining inside the tote with wrong side of lining toward inside of tote. Handstitch the folded edge to inside of tote.

Size:
About 12" tall x 11" wide without strap

Materials:
Worsted weight cotton yarn, 10 oz (500 yds, 300 g)
Optional for lining, 1/3 yd fabric
Size G aluminum crochet hook, or size required for gauge
One 1 1/2" diameter button
sewing needle and matching thread

Gauge:
4 dc = 1"

Instructions

Body
Ch 9.

Rnd 1 (right side):
Sc in 2nd ch from hook and in next 6 chs; 3 sc in next ch; working in unused lps on opposite side of beg ch, sc in next 6 lps, 2 sc in next lp; join in first sc—18 sc.

Rnd 2:
Ch 1, sc in same sc and in next 7 sc; 3 sc in next sc; sc in next 8 sc, 3 sc in next sc; join in first sc—22 sc.

Rnd 3:
Ch 1, sc in same sc and in next 7 sc; 2 sc in next sc; sc in next sc, 2 sc in next sc; sc in next 8 sc, 2 sc in next sc; sc in next sc, 2 sc in next sc; join in first sc—26 sc.

Rnd 4:
Ch 1, sc in same sc and in next 7 sc; † 2 sc in next sc; sc in next sc, 3 sc in next sc; sc in next sc, 2 sc in next sc †; sc in next 8 sc; rep from † to † once; join in first sc—34 sc.

Rnd 5:
Ch 1, sc in same sc and in next 9 sc; † 2 sc in next sc; sc in next sc, 3 sc in next sc; sc in next sc, 2 sc in next sc †; sc in next 12 sc; rep from † to † once; sc in next 2 sc; join in first sc—42 sc.

Rnd 6:
Ch 1, sc in same sc and in next 11 sc; † 2 sc in next sc; sc in next 3 sc, 2 sc in next sc †; sc in next 16 sc; rep from † to † once; sc in next 4 sc; join in first sc—46 sc.

Rnd 7:
Ch 1, sc in same sc and in next 13 sc; 2 sc in each of next 3 sc; sc in next 20 sc, 2 sc in each of next 3 sc; sc in next 6 sc; join in first sc—52 sc.

Rnd 8:
Ch 1, sc in same sc and in next 11 sc; † (2 sc in next sc, sc in next 3 sc) twice; 2 sc in next sc †; sc in next 17 sc; rep from † to † once; sc in next 5 sc; join in first sc—58 sc.

Rnd 9:
Ch 1, sc in same sc and in next 13 sc; † 2 sc in next sc; sc in next 3 sc, (2 sc in next sc, sc in next sc) twice; 2 sc in next sc; sc in next 3 sc, 2 sc in next sc †; sc in next 16 sc; rep from † to † once; sc in next 2 sc; join in first sc—68 sc.

Rnd 10:
Ch 1, sc in same sc and in next 16 sc; † (2 sc in next sc, sc in next 3 sc) twice; 2 sc in next sc †; sc in next 25 sc; rep from † to † once; sc in next 8 sc; join in first sc—74 sc.

Rnd 11:
Ch 1, sc in same sc and in next 19 sc; † (2 sc in next sc, sc in next 2 sc) twice; 2 sc in next sc †; sc in next 30 sc; rep from † to † once; sc in next 10 sc; join in first sc—80 sc.

Rnd 12:
Ch 1, sc in same sc and in each rem sc; join in first sc.

Rnd 13:
Rep Rnd 12.

Rnd 14:
Ch 2 (counts as an hdc), hdc in each sc; join in 2nd ch of beg ch-2. Finish off.

Rnd 15:
Make lp on hook and join with an sc in BL of 28th hdc from beg ch; working in BLs only, sc in each hdc and in joining sl st on prev rnd; join in joining sc—80 sc.

Rnd 16:
Ch 3, dc in each sc; join in 3rd ch of beg ch-3.

Rnd 17:
Sl st in next dc, ch 3, dc in joining sl st—beg X-st made; * sk next dc, dc in next dc, dc in skipped dc—X-st made; rep from * around; join in 3rd ch of beg ch-3—40 X-sts.

Rnd 18:
Ch 3, dc in each dc; join in 3rd ch of beg ch-3.

Rnd 19:
Ch 1, sc in same ch as joining and in each dc; join in BL of first sc.

Rnd 20:
Ch 1, sc in same lp as joining; working in BLs only, sc in each sc; join in first sc.

Rnds 21 through 35:
Rep Rnds 16 through 20 three times more.

Rnds 36 through 39:
Rep Rnds 16 through 19. At end of Rnd 39, finish off.

First Strap
Row 1 (right side):
Hold body with right side facing you and Rnd 39 at top; make lp on hook and join with an sc in BL of 3rd sc to right of joining on Rnd 39; sc in BL of next 10 sc—11 sc. Ch 1, turn, leaving rem sc unworked.

Row 2:
Dec over first 2 sc (to work dec: draw up lp in each of next 2 sc, YO and draw through all 3 lps on hook—dec made); sc in next 7 sc, dec over next 2 sc—9 sc. Ch 1, turn.

Row 3:
Dec; sc in next 5 sc, dec—7 sc. Ch 1, turn.

Row 4:
Dec; sc in next 3 sc, dec—5 sc. Ch 1, turn.

Row 5:
Sc in each sc. Ch 1, turn.

Rows 6 through 56:
Rep Row 5. At end of Row 56, do not ch 1. Finish off.

Flap
Row 1 (right side):
Hold body with right side facing you and Rnd 39 at top; make lp on hook and join with an sc in BL of first sc from first strap on Rnd 39; working in BLs only, sc in next 13 sc, dec; sc in next 13 sc—28 sc. Ch 2 (counts as first dc on following rows), turn, leaving rem sc unworked.

Row 2:
Dc in each sc. Ch 2, turn.

Row 3:
* Sk next dc, dc in next dc, dc in skipped dc; rep from * 12 times more; dc in 2nd ch of turning ch-2. Ch 2, turn.

Row 4:
Dc in each dc and in 2nd ch of turning ch-2. Ch 1, turn.

Row 5:
Sc in each dc and in 2nd ch of turning ch-2. Ch 1, turn.

Row 6:
Working in FLs only, sc in each sc. Ch 2, turn.

Row 7:
Dc in each sc. Finish off.

Row 8:
Join yarn in 2nd ch of turning ch; ch 2; * sk next dc, dc in next dc, dc in skipped dc; rep from * 12 times more; dc in next dc. Ch 2, turn.

Row 9:
Dc in each dc and in 2nd ch of beg ch-2. Ch 1, turn.

Row 10:
Sc in each dc and in 2nd ch of turning ch-2. Ch 1, turn.

continued

Row 11:
Working in FLs only, sc in each sc. Ch 2, turn.

Row 12:
Dc in each sc. Finish off.

Flap Trim:
Hold flap with wrong side facing you and Row 12 to left; make lp on hook and join with an sc in side of Row 1 of flap.

Row 1 (wrong side):
Working along side in sps formed by edge sts, (2 sc in each of next 3 rows, sc in next 2 rows) twice; sc in next row, working across Row 12, 3 sc in top of dc just worked; sc in next 26 dc, 3 sc in 2nd ch of turning ch-2; working along side in sps formed by edge sts, sc in sp formed by same turning ch as last 3 sc worked, (sc in next 2 rows, 2 sc in each of next 3 rows) twice; sc in next row. Ch 2, turn.

Row 2 (right side):
† Sk next sc, dc in next sc, dc in skipped sc †; rep from † to † 8 times more; 3 dc in next sc; rep from † to † 7 times; ch 6—button loop made; rep from † to † 7 times; 3 dc in next sc; rep from † to † 9 times; dc in next sc. Finish off.

Second Strap
Row 1 (right side):
Hold body with right side facing you and Rnd 39 at top; make lp on hook and join with an sc in BL of first sc from flap on Rnd 39; working in BLs only, sc in next 10 sc—11 sc. Ch 1, turn, leaving rem sc unworked.

Rows 2 through 56:
Rep Rows 2 through 56 of first strap. At end of Row 56, do not finish off.

Hold ends of straps with right sides together; working through both thicknesses, sl st through corresponding sc. Finish off.

Front Edge Strap Trim:
Hold tote with right side facing you and Rnd 39 at top; make lp on hook and join with an sc in BL of first sc from second strap on Rnd 39; working in BLs only, sc in next 29 sc, working along edge of strap in edge sc, sk Row 1, sc in Rows 2 through 56 of same strap and in Rows 56 through 2 of next strap, sk Row 1; join in first sc. Finish off.

Back Edge Strap Trim:
Hold tote with right side facing you and bottom of tote to right; make lp on hook and join with an sc in edge sc of Row 2 of second strap; working along edge of strap in edge sc, sc in Rows 3 through 56 of same strap and Rows 56 through 2 of next strap.

Finish off and weave in all ends.

Drawstring
Ch 150, sl st in 2nd ch from hook and in each rem ch.

Finish off and weave in ends.

Finishing
Step 1:
Referring to photo for placement, with sewing needle and matching thread, sew button to center front on Rnd 27.

Step 2:
Beginning and ending at center front, weave drawstring over and under cross stitches of Rnd 37.

Optional Lining
Step 1:
Cut a rectangle of lining fabric 10½" wide by 21" long. Cut an oval shape 6½" by 9½".

Step 2:
Place 10½" ends right sides together and sew with a ½" seam for side seam; press seam open.

Step 3:
Fold the oval in half and then fold again into quarters; mark each quarter along the edge. Also mark one open end of rectangle into quarters. Place lining pieces right sides together, matching the quarter marks; stitch with a ½" seam, easing rectangle to fit the oval.

Step 4:
On open edge, press ½" to the wrong side. Place lining inside the tote, ½" down from the top edge, with wrong side of lining toward inside of tote. Handstitch the folded edge to inside of tote.

Stylish
Shells

Casual Chic

In Vogue

In Bloom

Bands of
Beads

Jaunty Shells

Little Dashing Drawstring

Mini Duffle

Casual Chic

10

Stylish Shells

Bands of Beads

Mini Duffle

Little
Dashing Drawstring

In Bloom

In Bloom

In Vogue

Jaunty Shells

Casual Chic

Stylish Shells

Stylish Shells

Size:
About 16½" tall x 12½" wide without strap

Materials:
Worsted weight cotton yarn, 10 oz (500 yds, 300 g)
Optional for lining, ½ yd fabric; sewing needle and
  matching thread
Size G aluminum crochet hook, or size required
  for gauge
Size 16 tapestry needle

Gauge:
4 sc = 1"

Instructions

Body
Ch 4, join to form a ring.

Rnd 1 (right side):
Ch 1, 6 sc in ring; join in first sc.

Note: Rnds 2 through 43 are worked in continuous
rnds. Do not join; mark beg of rnds.

Rnd 2:
Ch 1, 2 sc in first sc and in each rem sc—12 sc.

Rnd 3:
(Sc in next sc, 2 sc in next sc) 6 times—18 sc.

Rnd 4:
(Sc in next 2 sc, 2 sc in next sc) 6 times—24 sc.

Rnd 5:
(Sc in next 3 sc, 2 sc in next sc) 6 times—30 sc.

Rnd 6:
(Sc in next 4 sc, 2 sc in next sc) 6 times—36 sc.

Rnd 7:
(Sc in next 5 sc, 2 sc in next sc) 6 times—42 sc.

Rnd 8:
(Sc in next 6 sc, 2 sc in next sc) 6 times—48 sc.

Rnd 9:
(Sc in next 7 sc, 2 sc in next sc) 6 times—54 sc.

Rnd 10:
(Sc in next 8 sc, 2 sc in next sc) 6 times—60 sc.

Rnd 11:
(Sc in next 9 sc, 2 sc in next sc) 6 times—66 sc.

Rnd 12:
(Sc in next 10 sc, 2 sc in next sc) 6 times—72 sc.

Rnd 13:
(Sc in next 5 sc, 2 sc in next sc) 12 times—84 sc.

Rnd 14:
Sc in each sc.

Rnd 15:
Sc in next 6 sc, 2 sc in next sc; (sc in next 13 sc, 2 sc in
next sc) 5 times; sc in next 7 sc—90 sc.

Rnd 16:
Sc in next sc, sk next sc, (3 dc in next sc, sk next sc, sc
in next sc, sk next sc) 22 times.

Rnd 17:
3 dc in next sc; sk next dc, (sc in next dc, sk next dc,
3 dc in next sc, sk next sc) 22 times.

Rnd 18:
Sc in next dc, sk next dc, (3 dc in next dc, sk next dc, sc
in next dc, sk next dc) 22 times.

Rnds 19 through 46:
Rep Rows 17 and 18 fourteen times. At end of Row 46,
join in first sc—twenty-two 3-dc groups.

First Strap

Row 1 (right side):
Sl st in next 2 dc, ch 1, sc in same dc as last sl st made;
(sk next dc, 3 dc in next dc, sk next dc, sc in next dc) 7
times. Turn, leaving rem sts unworked.

Row 2:
Sk first sc, sl st in next 2 dc, ch 1, sc in same dc as last
sl st made; (sk next dc, 3 dc in next dc, sk next dc, sc in
next dc) 6 times. Turn.

Row 3:
Sk first sc, sl st in next 2 dc, ch 1, sc in same dc as last
sl st made; (sk next dc, 3 dc in next dc, sk next dc, sc in
next dc) 5 times. Turn.

Row 4:
Sk first sc, sl st in next 2 dc, ch 1, sc in same dc as last
sl st made; (sk next dc, 3 dc in next dc, sk next dc, sc in
next dc) 4 times. Turn.

Row 5:
Sk first sc, sl st in next 2 dc, ch 1, sc in same dc as last
sl st made; (sk next dc, 3 dc in next dc, sk next dc, sc in
next dc) 3 times. Turn.

Row 6:
Sk first sc, sl st in next 2 dc, ch 1, sc in same dc as last
sl st made; (sk next dc, 3 dc in next dc, sk next dc, sc in
next dc) twice. Ch 1, turn.

Row 7:
Sc in first sc and in next 8 sts. Ch 1, turn.

Row 8:
Dec over first 2 sc (to work dec: draw up lp in each of
next 2 sc, YO and draw through all 3 lps on hook—dec
made); sc in next 5 sc, dec over next 2 sc—7 sc.
Ch 1, turn.

Row 9:
Sc in each sc. Ch 1, turn.

Rows 10 through 64:
Rep Row 9. At end of Row 64, finish off.

continued

Second Strap

Hold body with right side facing you and Rnd 46 at top; sk next 15 sts to left of first strap on Rnd 46; make lp on hook, join with an sc in next dc.

Row 1 (right side):
(Sk next dc, 3 dc in next sc, sk next dc, sc in next dc) 7 times. Turn, leaving rem sts unworked.

Rows 2 through 64:
Rep Rows 2 through 64 of first strap. At end of Row 64, do not finish off. Ch 1, turn.

Hold ends of straps with right sides together; working through both thicknesses, sl st through corresponding sc. Finish off.

Strap Edging

Hold body with right side facing you; make lp on hook and join with an sc in edge sc on Row 64 of one side of strap; working in sides of rows, sc in Rows 63 through 1; sc in each st on Rnd 46 of body, working across next side of strap, sc in Rows 1 through 64; join in joining sc. Finish off.

Work edging in same manner on opposite side of strap.

Weave in all ends.

Draw String (optional)

Ch 150, sl st in 2nd ch from hook and in each rem ch. Finish off, leaving a 6" end for weaving through bag. With tapestry needle and 6" end, beginning and ending at center front, weave drawstring over sc and under shells on Rnd 45 of body.

Weave in end.

Optional Lining
Step 1:
Cut a rectangle of lining fabric 12" wide by 27" long. Cut a circle 9" in diameter.

Step 2:
Place 12" ends right sides together and sew with a 1/2" seam for side seam; press seam open.

Step 3:
Fold the circle in half and then fold again into quarters; mark each quarter along the edge. Also mark one open end of rectangle into quarters. Place lining pieces right sides together, matching the quarter marks; stitch with a 1/2" seam easing rectangle to fit.

Step 4:
On open edge, press 1/2" to the wrong side. Place lining inside the tote below the drawstring with wrong side of lining toward inside of tote. Handstitch the folded edge to inside of tote.

Little Dashing Drawstring

Size:
About 10" tall x 8" wide without strap

Materials:
Worsted weight cotton yarn, 2½ oz (125 yds, 75 g) each for two color version
Note: Solid color version, 5 oz (250 yds, 150 g)
Optional for lining, ¼ yd fabric; sewing needle and matching thread
Size G aluminum crochet hook, or size required for gauge
one 25mm wooden bead

Gauge:
4 hdc = 1"
3 hdc rows = 1"

Instructions
Note: Directions are written with color changes. If a solid color tote is desired, disregard color changes.

Body
Starting at bottom with main color, ch 2.

Rnd 1 (right side):
6 sc in 2nd ch from hook; join in first sc—6 sc.

Rnd 2:
Ch 3 (counts as a dc on this and following rnds), dc in same sc; 2 dc in each rem sc; join in 3rd ch of beg ch-3—12 dc.

Rnd 3:
Ch 3, dc in same ch as joining; 2 dc in each dc; join in 3rd ch of beg ch-3—24 dc.

Rnd 4:
Ch 3, 2 dc in next dc; (dc in next dc, 2 dc in next dc) 11 times; join in 3rd ch of beg ch-3—36 dc.

Rnd 5:
Ch 3, dc in next dc, 2 dc in next dc; (dc in next 2 dc, 2 dc in next dc) 11 times; join in 3rd ch of beg ch-3—48 dc.

Rnd 6:
Ch 1, sc in same ch as joining and in next 2 dc, 2 sc in next dc; (sc in next 3 dc, 2 sc in next dc) 11 times; join in first sc—60 dc.

Rnd 7:
Ch 2, hdc in each sc; join in 2nd ch of beg ch-2. Change to second color by drawing lp through; cut main color.

Rnd 8:
Ch 2, hdc in each hdc; join in 2nd ch of beg ch-2.

Rnds 9 and 10:
Rep Rnd 8.

Rnd 11:
Ch 2, hdc in each hdc; join in 2nd ch of beg ch-2. Change to main color by drawing lp through; cut second color.

Rnd 12:
Rep Rnd 8.

Rnd 13:
Ch 2, hdc in each hdc; join in 2nd ch of beg ch-2. Change to second color by drawing lp through; cut main color.

Rnds 14 through 19:
Rep Rnds 8 through 13.

Rnds 20 through 24:
Rep Rnds 8 through 12.

Rnd 25 (drawstring rnd):
Ch 4 (counts as a dc and a ch-1 sp), sk next hdc, (dc in next hdc, ch 1, sk next hdc) 29 times; join in 3rd ch of beg ch-4. Change to second color by drawing lp through; cut main color.

Rnd 26:
Ch 2, hdc in each ch-1 sp and in each dc; join in 2nd ch of beg ch-2—60 dc.

Rnd 27:
Rep Rnd 8.

Rnd 28:
Ch 1, sc in same ch as joining and in each hdc; join in first sc. Finish off.

Strap

With second color, ch 195 to measure about 48" long; hold body with right side facing you and Rnd 28 at top and fold Rnds 26, 27 and 28 toward you; sl st from back to front to back around post (see Stitch Guide on page 2) of 8th dc from joining on Rnd 25—strap joining; ch 1, turn; sc in each ch; hold right side of body facing you and Rnd 28 at top and fold Rnds 26, 27 and 28 toward you, being careful not to twist ch; sl st from back to front to back around post of 15th dc from strap joining on Rnd 25.

Finish off and weave in all ends.

Drawstring:

With main color, ch 120 to measure about 30" long; sc in 2nd ch from hook and in each rem ch. Finish off and weave in ends. Beginning and ending in ch-1 sp between 15th and 16th dc on Rnd 25, weave drawstring over and under each dc. Hold ends together and pull each length even, insert the ends through center of wooden bead; tie each end into a knot.

Optional Lining

Step 1:
Cut a rectangle of lining fabric 7" wide by 16" long. Cut a circle 6" in diameter.

Step 2:
Place 7" ends right sides together and sew with a $\frac{1}{2}$" seam for side seam; press seam open.

Step 3:
Fold the circle in half and then fold again into quarters; mark each quarter along the edge. Also mark one open end of rectangle into quarters. Place lining pieces right sides together, matching the quarter marks; stitch with a $\frac{1}{2}$" seam, easing rectangle to fit.

Step 4:
On open edge, press $\frac{1}{2}$" to the wrong side. Place lining inside the tote, below the drawstring, with wrong side of lining toward inside of tote. Handstitch the folded edge to inside of tote.

Size:
About 17" tall x 12" wide without strap

Materials:
Worsted weight cotton yarn, 13 oz (650 yds, 390 g)
Optional for lining, 1/3 yd fabric; sewing needle and matching thread
Size G aluminum crochet hook, or size required for gauge
Size 16 tapestry needle

Gauge:
4 dc = 1"

Pattern Stitch

Back Post Single Crochet (BPsc):
Insert hook from back to front to back around post (see Stitch Guide on page 2) of next sc on second row below, YO, draw lp through, YO and draw through 2 lps on hook—BPsc made.

Instructions

Square (make 12)
Ch 2.

Rnd 1 (right side):
8 sc in 2nd ch from hook; join in first sc.

Rnd 2:
Ch 1, sc in same sc; ch 3, (sc in next sc, ch 3) 7 times; do not join—8 ch-3 sps.

Rnd 3:
In next ch-3 sp work (sc, hdc, dc, trc, dc, hdc, sc)—petal made; in each rem ch-3 sp work (sc, hdc, dc, trc, dc, hdc, sc)—petal made; join in first sc—8 petals made.

Rnd 4:
Ch 4, working behind petals of Rnd 3, [BPsc (see Pattern Stitch) around next sc on Rnd 2, ch 4] 7 times; join in beg ch-4 sp.

Rnd 5:
Ch 3 (counts as a dc on this and following rnds), 4 dc in same sp; ch 1, (5 dc in next ch-4 sp, ch 1) 7 times; join in 3rd ch of beg ch-3—eight 5-dc groups.

Rnd 6:
Sl st in next 2 dc, ch 3, in same dc work (2 dc, ch 3, 3 dc)—beg corner made; * in next ch-1 sp work (dc, ch 1, dc); sc in 3rd dc of next 5-dc group, in next ch-1 sp work (dc, ch 1, dc); in 3rd dc of next 5-dc group work (3 dc, ch 3, 3 dc)—corner made; rep from * twice more; in next ch-1 sp work (dc, ch 1, dc); sc in 3rd dc of next 5-dc group, in next ch-1 sp work (dc, ch 1, dc); join in 3rd ch of beg ch-3.

Rnd 7:
Ch 1, sc in same ch as joining and in next 2 dc, 3 sc in next corner ch-3 sp; working in each dc, in each ch-1 sp and in each sc, * sc in next 13 sts, 3 sc in next corner ch-3 sp; rep from * twice more; sc in next 10 sts; join in first sc.

Finish off and weave in ends.

Joining Squares

Join squares in two rows of 6 squares each. To join squares, hold two squares with right sides together; using tapestry needle and overcast st (see Stitch Guide on page 2), sew squares together in BLs only, leaving 2nd sc of 3-sc corner groups unworked. Repeat with remaining squares.

Join rows together in same manner, joining 2nd sc of corners. Sew ends of rows together to form a circle. Join in 2nd sc of 3-sc corner groups, leave top and bottom unworked. Weave in all ends.

Bottom

Hold circle with right side facing you; make lp on hook and join with an sc in joining between any two squares.

Rnd 1 (right side):
Working in BLs of sc, sc in each sc and in each joining; join in first sc—108 sc.

Rnd 2:
Ch 1, sc in same sc and in next 6 sc; dec over next 2 sc (to work dec: draw up lp in each of next 2 sc, YO and draw through all 3 lps on hook—dec made); (sc in next 7 sc, dec over next 2 sc) 11 times; join in first sc—96 sc.

Rnd 3:
Ch 1, sc in same sc and in next 5 sc; dec; (sc in next 6 sc, dec) 11 times; join in BL of first sc—84 sc.

Rnd 4:
Ch 1, sc in same lp as joining; working in BLs only, sc in each sc; join in first sc.

Rnd 5:
Ch 1, sc in same sc and in next 4 sc; dec; (dc in next 5 dc, dec) 11 times; join in first sc—72 sc.

Rnd 6:
Ch 1, sc in same sc and in next 9 sc; dec; (sc in next 10 sc, dec) 5 times; join in first sc—66 sc.

Rnd 7:
Ch 1, sc in same sc and in next 8 sc; dec; (sc in next 9 sc, dec) 5 times; join in first sc—60 sc.

Rnd 8:
Ch 1, sc in same sc and in next 7 sc, dec; (sc in next 8 sc, dec) 5 times; join in first sc—54 sc.

Rnd 9:
Ch 1, sc in same sc and in next 6 sc; dec; (sc in next 7 sc, dec) 5 times; join in first sc—48 sc.

Rnd 10:
Ch 1, sc in same sc and in next 5 sc; dec; (sc in next 6 sc, dec) 5 times; join in first sc—42 sc.

Rnd 11:
Ch 1, sc in same sc and in next 4 sc; dec; (sc in next 5 sc, dec) 5 times; join in first sc—36 sc.

Rnd 12:
Ch 1, sc in same sc and in next 3 sc; dec; (sc in next 4 sc, dec) 5 times; join in first sc—30 sc.

Rnd 13:
Ch 1, sc in same sc and in next 2 sc; dec; (sc in next 3 sc, dec) 5 times; join in first sc—24 sc.

Rnd 14:
Ch 1, sc in same sc and in next sc; dec; (sc in next 2 sc, dec) 5 times; join in first sc—18 sc.

Rnd 15:
Ch 1, sc in same sc; dec; (sc in next sc, dec) 5 times; join in first sc—12 sc.

Rnd 16:
Ch 1, dec 6 times; join in first sc—6 sc.

Finish off, leaving a 12" end for sewing. Thread yarn into tapestry needle; weave through tops of sc on Rnd 16 to gather. Pull tight and weave in end.

Top
Hold piece with right side facing you and unworked edge of circle at top; make lp on hook and join with an sc in joining of any two squares.

Note: Rnds 1 thorugh 5 are worked in continuous rnds. Do not join; make beg of rnds.

Rnd 1 (right side):
Working in BLs of sc, sc in each sc and in each join-ing—108 sc.

Rnd 2:
Sc in each sc.

Rnds 3 through 6:
Rep Rnd 2. At end of Rnd 6, join in first sc. Ch 1, turn.

Front Top Shaping:
Row 1 (wrong side):
Sc in next 49 sc. Ch 1, turn, leaving rem sc unworked.

Row 2 (right side):
Sc in first sc, dec; sc to last 3 sc; dec; sc in last sc—47 sc. Ch 1, turn.

Rows 3 through 22:
Rep Row 2. At end of Row 22—7 sc.

Row 23:
Sc in each sc. Ch 1, turn.

Rows 24 through 67:
Rep Row 23. At end of Row 67, do not ch 1. Finish off.

Back Top Shaping:
Hold piece with wrong side facing you; make lp on hook and join with an sc in 6th unused sc from front top shaping.

Work same as front top shaping. At end of Row 67, ch 1, turn.

Hold ends of straps with right sides together; working through both thicknesses, sl st through corresponding sc. Finish off.

Strap Edging
Hold tote with right side facing you; make lp on hook and join with an sc in edge sc on Row 67 of one side of strap; working in sides of rows, sc in Rows 66 through 1; working across top edge of tote, sc in next 5 sc on Rnd 6; working along side of next strap in sides of rows, sc in Rows 1 through 67; join in joining sc.

Work edging in same manner on opposite side of strap.

Weave in all ends.

Finishing
Lightly steam flower petals on squares to make them lie flat.

Optional Lining
Step 1:
Cut rectangle of lining fabric 10" wide by 27" long. Cut a circle 10" in diameter.

Step 2:
Place 10" ends right sides together and sew with a 1/2" seam for side seam; press seam open.

Step 3:
Fold circle in half and then fold again into quarters; mark each quarter along the edge. Also mark one open end of rectangle into quarters. Place lining pieces right sides together, matching the quarter marks; stitch with a 1/2" seam, easing rectangle to fit.

Step 4:
On open edge, press 1/2" to the wrong side. Place lining inside the tote 1/2" down from side top edges, with wrong side of lining toward inside of tote. Handstitch the folded edge to inside of tote.

Mini Duffle

Size:
About 17" tall x 14" wide

Materials:
Worsted weight cotton yarn, 13 oz (650 yds, 390 g)
Optional for lining, ½ yd fabric; sewing needle and matching thread
Size G aluminum crochet hook, or size required for gauge

Gauge:
4 dc = 1"
2 dc rnds = 1"
3 FC = 1"
2 FC rows = 1"

Pattern Stitch

Forked Cluster (FC):
YO, draw up lp in st indicated, YO, draw up lp in next st indicated (5 lps on hook), (YO and draw through 3 lps on hook) twice—FC made.

Instructions

Body
Ch 4, join to form a ring.

Rnd 1 (right side):
Ch 3 (counts as a dc on this and following rnds), 9 dc in ring; join in 3rd ch of beg ch-3—10 dc.

Rnd 2:
Ch 3, dc in same ch as joining; 2 dc in each dc; join in 3rd ch of beg ch-3—20 dc.

Rnd 3:
Ch 3, 2 dc in next dc; (dc in next dc, 2 dc in next dc) 9 times; join in 3rd ch of beg ch-3—30 dc.

Rnd 4:
Ch 3, dc in same ch as joining; dc in next 2 dc, (2 dc in next dc, dc in next 2 dc) 9 times; join in 3rd ch of beg ch-3—40 dc.

Rnd 5:
Ch 3, dc in next dc, (2 dc in next dc, dc in next 3 dc) 9 times; 2 dc in next dc; dc in next dc; join in 3rd ch of beg ch-3—50 dc.

Rnd 6:
Ch 3, dc in next 2 dc, (2 dc in next dc, dc in next 4 dc) 9 times; 2 dc in next dc; dc in next dc; join in 3rd ch of beg ch-3—60 dc.

Rnd 7:
Ch 3, dc in next 3 dc, (2 dc in next dc, dc in next 5 dc) 9 times; 2 dc in next dc; dc in next dc; join in 3rd ch of beg ch-3—70 dc.

Rnd 8:
Ch 3, dc in next 4 dc, (2 dc in next dc, dc in next 6 dc) 9 times; 2 dc in next dc; dc in next dc; join in 3rd ch of beg ch-3—80 dc.

Rnd 9:
Ch 3, dc in next 5 dc, (2 dc in next dc, dc in next 7 dc) 9 times; 2 dc in next dc; dc in next dc; join in 3rd ch of beg ch-3—90 dc.

Rnd 10:
Ch 3 (mark ch 3 for strap placement), dc in next 6 dc, (2 dc in next dc, dc in next 8 dc) 9 times; 2 dc in next dc; dc in next dc; join in 3rd ch of beg ch-3—100 dc.

Note: Rnds 11 through 31 are worked in continuous rnds. Do not join; mark beg of each rnd.

Rnd 11:
Ch 3, FC (see Pattern Stitch) in same ch as joining and in next dc; * FC in same dc as last FC worked and in next dc; rep from * 97 times; FC in same dc as last FC worked and in first FC—100 FCs.

Rnd 12:
* FC in last FC worked and in next FC; rep from * around.

Rnds 13 through 30:
Rep Rnd 12.

Rnd 31 (draw string rnd):
FC in last FC worked and in next FC; ch 2; * FC over next 2 FCs; ch 2; rep from * around—50 ch-2 sps.

Strap
Row 1:
Sk next FC, sl st in next ch-2 sp, ch 80, sl st in 3rd ch of beg ch-3 on Rnd 10 (marked ch-3 already worked). Ch 1, turn.

Row 2:
Sc in each ch and in same ch-2 sp as ch-80 worked. Ch 1, turn.

Row 3:
Sc in each sc and in next dc on Rnd 10 (already worked). Ch 1, turn.

Row 4:
Sc in each sc and in same ch-2 sp as joining sc on Row 2. Ch 1, turn.

Row 5:
Sc in each sc and in next dc on Rnd 10 (already worked). Turn.

Row 6:
Sl st loosely in each sc and in previously worked ch-2 sp.

Top of Bag
Rnd 1 (right side):
Sl st in next FC, ch 3 (counts as a dc on this and following rnds), dc in each ch-2 sp and in each FC to strap joining; working in next ch-2 sp already worked, dc between joinings of Rows 3 and 4 of strap and between joinings of Rows 4 and 5 of strap; join in 3rd ch of beg ch-3.

Rnd 2:
Ch 3, dc in each dc; join in 3rd ch of beg ch-3.

Rnd 3:
Rep Rnd 2.

Finish off and weave in all ends.

Drawstring
Ch 200, sl st in 2nd ch from hook and in each rem ch. Finish off and weave in ends. Beginning and ending in ch-2 sp between 24th and 25th FC on Rnd 31, weave drawstring over and under FCs.

Optional Lining
Step 1:
Cut a rectangle of lining fabric 11½" wide by 31" long. Cut a circle 10" in diameter.

Step 2:
Place 11½" ends right sides together and sew a ½" seam for side seam; press seam open.

Step 3:
Fold the circle in half and then fold again into quarters; mark each quarter along the edge. Also mark one open end of rectangle into quarters. Place lining pieces right sides together, matching the quarter marks; stitch with a ½" seam easing rectangle to fit.

Step 4:
On open edge, press ½" to the wrong side. Place lining inside the tote below the drawstring, with wrong side of lining toward inside of tote. Handstitch the folded edge to inside of tote.

 Bands of Beads

Size:
About 20" tall x 15" wide without strap

Materials:
Worsted weight cotton yarn, 15 oz (750 yds, 450 g)
Optional for lining, ½ yd fabric; sewing needle and matching thread
Size G aluminum crochet hook, or size required for gauge
378— 6x9mm multi-colored pony beads
Size 16 tapestry needle

Gauge:
4 hdc = 1"
3 hdc rows = 1"

Instructions

Body
Thread (at least 54 beads on first ball of yarn) 378 beads onto yarn. Thread 108 beads on second ball of yarn. Thread 162 beads on third ball of yarn and thread rem beads on fourth ball of yarn.

Note: Slide beads aside until needed.

Ch 4, join to form a ring.

Rnd 1 (right side):
Ch 1, 6 sc in ring; join in first sc.

Note: Rnds 2 through 20 are worked in continuous rnds. Do not join; mark beg of rnds.

Rnds 2 through 13:
Rep Rnds 2 through 13 on Shell Tote (see page 13).

Rnd 14:
(Sc in next 6 sc, 2 sc in next sc) 12 times—96 sc.

Rnd 15:
(Sc in next 7 sc, 2 sc in next sc) 12 times—108 sc.

Rnd 16:
Sc in each sc.

Rnd 17:
Hdc in each sc.

Rnd 18:
Hdc in each hdc.

Rnd 19:
Hdc in next 107 hdc, sl st in next hdc.

Rnd 20:
Sl st in next hdc, ch 4 (counts as a dc and a ch-1 sp on this and following rnds), move one bead up to hook, ch 1, sk next hdc; * dc in next hdc, ch 1, move one bead up to hook, ch 1, sk next hdc; rep from * 52 times more; join in 3rd ch of beg ch-4—54 dc.

Rnd 21:
Ch 2 (counts as and hdc on this and following rnds), hdc in lp over each bead and in each dc; join in 2nd ch of beg ch-2—108 hdc.

Rnd 22:
Ch 2, hdc in each hdc; join in 2nd ch of beg ch-2.

Rnds 23 and 24:
Rep Rnd 22.

Rnds 25 through 54:
Rep Rnds 20 through 24 six times more.

First Half of Top Shaping and Strap
Row 1 (right side):
Ch 1, sc in same ch as joining and in next 51 hdc—52 sc. Ch 1, turn, leaving rem hdc unworked.

Row 2:
Sc in first sc, dec over next 2 sc (to work dec: draw up lp in next 2 sc, YO and draw through all 3 lps on hook—dec made); sc in next 46 sc, dec over next 2 sc; sc in next sc—50 sc. Ch 1, turn.

Row 3:
Sc in first sc, dec; sc in each sc to last 3 sc, dec; sc in next sc—48 sc. Ch 1, turn.

Rows 4 through 24:
Rep Row 3. At end of Row 24—6 sc. Ch 1, turn.

Row 25:
Sc in each sc. Ch 1, turn.

Rows 26 through 67:
Rep Row 25. At end of Row 67, do not ch 1. Finish off.

Second Half of Top Shaping and Strap
Hold body with right side facing you and Rnd 54 at top; sk next 2 hdc from first strap on body, make lp on hook and join with an sc in next hdc.

Row 1 (right side):
Sc in next 51 hdc—52 sc. Ch 1, turn, leaving rem 2 hdc unworked.

Rows 2 through 67:
Rep Rows 2 through 67 on first half of top shaping and strap. At end of Row 67, do not finish off. Ch 1, turn.

Hold ends of straps with right sides together; working through both thicknesses, sl st through corresponding sc. Finish off.

Strap Edging
Hold body with right side facing you; make lp on hook and join with an sc in edge sc on Row 67 of one strap; working in sides of rows, sc in Rows 66 through 1, working across top edge of body, sc in next 2 hdc on Rnd 54, working is sides of rows on next strap, sc in Rows 1 through 67; join in joining sc. Finish off.